Eco Gardening
FOR EVERYONE

INTRODUCTION

This book is all about doing something positive (a great many things in actual fact). It's easy to get depressed in the face of dire predictions about global warming, the destruction of fragile ecosystems and the loss of essential resources. But eco gardening is about taking steps at home – in the garden – to make significant changes.

Eco gardening calls on the experience and know-how of organic gardening and the wider ecological movement. It encourages us to grow tasty and nourishing fruit and vegetables in a natural way that is efficient and productive – without the need to use chemicals to promote plant growth or combat pests and diseases. At the same time, eco gardening shows us how to reuse and recycle lots of things that might otherwise be thrown away: garden refuse that can be turned into soil-improving compost; empty yogurt pots which make ideal containers for seedlings; plastic bottles as mini-cloches.

This kind of creative, clear-sighted approach helps us understand the wider implications of using, in the garden, resources and materials that are easily taken for granted. Why not save money on electricity or petrol by mowing the lawn with a hand push cylinder mower? How about saving rainwater to use on our plants? And where will rainwater go after it falls on the patio with a solid surface that we're thinking of building? Then there are those concrete slabs we have in mind – how much energy has been used to make them and deliver them to us? These are the kind of considerations and solutions that eco gardening brings to the fore.

At its core it highlights the importance of working with nature. Encouraging birds, insects, small mammals, reptiles and amphibians to visit our gardens will deliver a

▶ 'The Rain Chain' garden which won the Best Sustainable Garden at the RHS Hampton Court Palace Flower Show in 2009 . The designer, Wendy Allen, said, 'We believe sustainable design does not have to be strawbales and recycled wellies, although we like them too.'

range of natural predators to help keep down plant-damaging pests.

Nature also gives a lead in garden design and plant selection. It may seem obvious, but choosing plants that will prosper in the soil and situation of a particular garden will result in far more satisfactory results than trying to coax plants to grow in conditions to which they are unsuited.

Putting ideas like this into practice may look like a challenge, but when the benefits of eco gardening are so heavily stacked in their favour it's a challenge well worth accepting. That's where this book is ready to lend a hand in getting us started.

BIODIVERSITY

Biodiversity is a word that crops up a lot in discussions about the environment, ecosystems and the threats posed to the 'balance of nature'. But what exactly does it mean?

You could say that it is the variety of everything living on earth: plants, animals, micro-organisms. But biodiversity goes further than simply acknowledging that the world is full of an amazing array of species. It highlights the importance of the subtle differences that exist among them. Every slight variation between one member of a plant or animal group and the rest gives it a unique quality that could enable it to survive should the others suffer a decline.

Tempting as it may be to focus on a single vegetable variety, for example, that grows successfully with good yields, this kind of monoculture can be risky. It only takes a virulent pest or disease to attack that one variety and the entire crop could be lost. But if a range of varieties is grown, there is a chance that some might fare better if disease or pests strike, at least ensuring that part of the crop survives.

For the eco gardener, focused on developing a healthy and sustainable system of plant propagation and food production, biodiversity is a key goal – and it isn't restricted to plants. By encouraging a wide variety of wildlife into a garden, the eco gardener gains the support of a great many different creatures that perform a multitude of tasks. Some, like worms and microbes in the ground, work away at improving the soil. Beneficial insects, drawn to a garden by the kinds of plants they like to feed on, produce larvae that prey on aphids. Many birds perform important pest-control tasks too: thrushes devouring snails; blue tits consuming plant-damaging caterpillars. Then there are wildlife visitors who devour slugs – frogs and

▶ Putting up nesting boxes to suit birds of differing sizes will encourage a variety of birds to nest and raise their young in your garden – the benefit of their presence will vary but the adult birds will often feed their young on garden visitors that you would prefer to see gobbled up.

hedgehogs among others. The greater the variety of wildlife in a garden, the more useful things they can do to help a gardener. Added to this is the growing importance of gardens in providing habitats and sources of food that are being lost elsewhere – in intensively farmed parts of the country as well as built-up areas.

For the eco gardener, maintaining and increasing biodiversity in a garden isn't an optional extra. It may only be a tiny part in a global movement, but like many aspects of eco gardening it is a small step in the right direction and when a lot of gardeners take a step, they develop momentum and things start to change – for the better, for everyone, everywhere.

WILDLIFE-FRIENDLY GARDENS

Gardeners who make their gardens more wildlife friendly benefit from the increase in natural predators – taking on a significant part of pest-control that might formerly have been performed by pesticides. This reduces the amount of chemicals used in the garden.

For the nation as a whole, wildlife-friendly gardens are becoming increasingly important in providing diverse habitats for a significant number of birds and other creatures. According to The Big Wildlife Garden (www.bigwildlifegarden.org.uk), promoted by the Royal Horticultural Society and The Wildlife Trusts, the 19 million or so gardens in the UK cover an area well in excess of all the national nature reserves added together.

Increasing the wildlife activity in an existing garden simply amounts to incorporating a few of the basic requirements for the creatures that we want to attract.

- Something to eat
- Something to drink
- Somewhere to live and breed securely

It is also important to offer a variety of food supplies and habitats to attract a wide cross-section of wildlife and to offer them all year round.

WELCOMING WILDLIFE

Four valuable ways of boosting wildlife activity in a garden to tackle plant-damaging pests.

- Install a pond to provide drinking water for wildlife visitors and a habitat for insects and amphibians such as frogs, which feed on slugs.

- Grow trees and fruit-bearing shrubs where birds and insects can find shelter and food.

- Stock beds with plants that collectively give the longest flowering season, to give birds, bees and other beneficial insects sources of food for as long as possible.

- Create year-round wildlife safe havens – piles of wood, mixed hedges, climbing plants – that will provide food and shelter for amphibians, insects and mammals.

UNTIDY HOMES

Wildlife visitors will feel at home in gardens that themselves feel 'wild'. Leaving areas of a garden untidy to the human eye will make them desirable to many different kinds of creature. Damp, sheltered hideaways such as a pile of logs or a heap of decaying leaves will appeal to frogs, newts and hedgehogs.

Hedges are ideal habitats for many pest-eaters. For this reason hedge trimming should be

delayed until the second half of the summer, by which time birds nesting in the hedge will have finished rearing their young, although hedges with fruiting plants such as hawthorn and blackthorn ought not to be trimmed until garden birds have had their fill of the berries.

There is no need to throw away or compost hedge trimmings immediately. Put in a corner, these can provide shelter for creatures ranging from hedgehogs to beetles and other insects.

Keeping an area of grass uncut will enable wild flowers and grasses to flower and set seed, creating what amounts to a meadow in miniature. This is the kind of habitat that appeals to many kinds of insect.

AN UNDISTURBED PILE OF ROTTING LOGS IS A HAVEN FOR CREATURES LIKE BEETLES, FROGS AND HEDGEHOGS THAT LIKE COOL, DARK PLACES IN WHICH TO SHELTER

HEDGEHOGS' HOME FROM HOME

Although hedgehogs are widely credited with devouring slugs and snails, they will eat practically anything that comes their way. Research published on the website Hedgehog Bottom Rescue (www.hedgehog-rescue.org.uk) indicates that slugs and snails probably account for around 5% of a hedgehog's diet, while insects and beetles make up over 70%. That said, any creature prepared to eat slugs and snails at all is welcome in the garden.

In the first instance a hedgehog needs to be able to get into a garden, so small gaps in the bottom of fences, strategically located in sheltered parts of the garden (under a hedge or other dense foliage) will help it gain access. Once in the garden it will need somewhere to live. Buy a ready-made hedgehog box (or make your own) and hide it under a pile of leaves. A small pile of hay left close by might encourage a hedgehog to build a nest inside and take up residence. On the other hand, one of the natural homes described earlier could serve a hedgehog just as well.

The key point to remember about these is always to check whether a hedgehog has decided to move in before you disturb a pile of leaves or any other 'untidy' heap that has been left untouched for a while. This is particularly important with piles of garden rubbish that you might be thinking of burning. Setting fire to any pile of garden rubbish without first checking if a hedgehog or any other creature is living in it effectively signs their death warrant. Try and hold off until the spring before lighting a bonfire – once the hibernating season is over – but even then it's worth taking a good peek in your pile.

▼ The UK hedgehog population has dropped by a quarter in the last 10 years and hedgehogs need all the help they can get. The British Hedgehog Preservation Society (website details at the end of the book) gives guidance if you find a hedgehog in distress.

THE FOX HAS MANY TRICKS. THE HEDGEHOG HAS BUT ONE. BUT THAT IS THE BEST OF ALL.

RALPH WALDO EMERSON

BIRDS

Birds are one of the eco gardener's most important allies in combating pests that damage growing plants, and therefore play a key role in reducing the use of garden chemicals. Their contribution can be substantial – it has been estimated that one pair of blue tits, for example, can consume upwards of 7,000 caterpillars in the course of feeding an average-sized brood.

Birds can be encouraged into a garden if they are provided with nesting sites, water, berried shrubs supplemented with food in winter, and perching sites where they are safe from predators.

A hedge of mixed native species will offer sheltered places for nesting birds. So will the dense foliage of plants like holly and ivy, which provide welcome winter shelter for varieties of small birds like wrens and tits.

A lot of gardens may lack suitable places for birds to nest and this is where nesting boxes are an ideal substitute for naturally occurring holes in trees. Bird boxes should be sited away from

direct sunlight, with their entrances sheltered from driven rain and ideally about 1.5m above the ground (an exception being open-fronted boxes mentioned overleaf). You need to think about cats too, positioning a nesting box where it is safe from the marauding moggies. But don't make it too difficult for you to reach yourself, because you'll need to take it down every autumn for cleaning and any repairs.

Different birds will be attracted to boxes with different-sized points of access. Those with a circular hole in the front panel will be occupied by birds according to their size. RSPB guidelines advise the following:

FRUIT AND BERRIES FOR BIRDS

The RSPB includes the following in its list of fruit- and berry-bearing trees or bushes to attract a range of wild birds:

- Berberis
- Cotoneaster
- Dog rose
- Elder
- Guelder rose
- Hawthorn
- Holly
- Honeysuckle
- Ivy
- Pyracantha
- Rowan
- Spindle
- Whitebeam

13

- 25mm hole for birds such as blue tits
- 28mm hole for birds such as great tits
- 32mm hole for birds such as house sparrows
- 45mm hole for starlings

Open-fronted boxes (positioned low down in thick foliage) are occupied by other birds, depending on the height of the opening:

- 60mm opening for spotted flycatchers
- 100mm opening for robins
- 140mm opening for wrens

A pond (described in detail later in the book) will supply drinking and bathing water for garden birds, but failing that a birdbath, kept clean and well topped up, is a good substitute. You'll need to remember to remove any ice that forms on the surface of your water supply, so that birds can still get at the water.

Although birds appreciate food supplied by us all year round, winter is when they most need human support. Suspended bird feeders, in the right place, stocked with a selection of seeds, nuts and fat, give birds dry food and somewhere they can feed while sheltered from prevailing winds.

Bird tables are convenient feeding areas too, although watch out for cats preying on the birds and squirrels trying to steal their food.

As soon as plant predators begin to flourish, the birds that prey on them will add aphids, caterpillars, insects, slugs, snails and other pests to their diet. When wild berries and fruits begin to ripen, birds will be able to feast on these too, giving a further incentive for some of them to decide to spend the winter in a garden – along with suitable accommodation and a constant supply of water.

Many garden birds gorge on sunflower seeds, so growing your own sunflowers is an obvious source of 'home-made' bird food. Either leave the flower heads in place, or cut them off and hang them in a suitable place in order for the birds to benefit from the seed as it matures and dries.

BATS

Bats work the 'night shift' for eco gardeners. They feed on moths, some of which (codling moth, leek moth, pea moth for example) produce larvae that damage plants. Bats also feed on midges and mosquitoes, which can be a nuisance when you're sitting outside on warm summer nights.

With the numbers of bats declining, legislative and environmental measures have been put in place to look after them and their habitats. Eco gardeners can make an important contribution towards maintaining and ideally increasing bat populations.

Bats will find places to roost in sheltered nooks and crannies: in eaves, under tiles, in tree hollows. They will also take up residence in small bat boxes. These look similar to enclosed bird boxes, except that the entrance is formed by a slit in the base rather than a hole in the front or side panel. As a protected species bats must not be disturbed and bat boxes should be positioned at least three metres above ground level, in a warm sunny location away from human activity and household pets. Here they will live during the warm months of the year before finding somewhere secluded and sheltered (crevices in trees, or quiet corners of empty buildings) to hibernate for the winter.

▼ The best place to position a bat box is on a tree. Ideally place them in groups round three sides of a tree as bats like to move from one box to another during the day, and from season to season as temperatures change.

BEES' NEEDS

Bees are friends to every gardener and they are essential for our ecosystem. There is an oft-quoted statistic attributed to Albert Einstein, which claims that if bees disappeared entirely mankind would only have four years to live.

It is questionable whether Einstein actually said that and apocalyptic statements like this greatly exaggerate a complex issue. What is undeniable is that almost one third of world farming requires animals to pollinate crops and approaching 90% of that pollination is done by honey bees.

These stark figures explain why the decline in wild colonies and the threat posed by viruses and disease to bees kept in hives is a cause of major concern worldwide. They also show how gardeners who attract bees into their gardens serve the wider gardening and agricultural community, as well as the propagation of their own plants.

Bees will make themselves at home in a variety of different places. Honey bees are social bees that live in colonies situated in hives. Bumble bees find homes in holes in the ground, often taking over those burrowed by mice or other rodents. Solitary bees, like the mason bees that pollinate orchards, usually live in holes in the ground, although they will find habitats in

COMMON WILD FLOWERS FOR BEES

- Bird's foot trefoil
- Clover (red and white)
- Dandelion – but pick off the flowers before they form their 'clock' or else you will have a garden full of dandelions
- Dead nettle
- Dog rose
- Thistle

▲ You don't necessarily need to become a beekeeper to help keep bees. Now you can share in the hidden world of the honey bee by adopting a beehive through the British Beekeepers Association http://www.bbka.org.uk/about/adopt_a_beehive.

hollow plant stems as well as man-made homes created from blocks of wood drilled with holes, or straws packed inside a waterproof container. Purpose-made bee boxes also contribute valuable garden accommodation for bees.

As winter approaches, some bees will seek out refuges sheltered from wind and rain where they can hibernate. Others will find holes in the ground, or hollows in trees into which to retreat. Honey bees clump together in a constantly vibrating cluster centred on the queen. The majority of British honey bees live in managed hives, where each colony forms a cluster similar in size and shape to a rugby ball.

Bees feed on pollen and nectar, so it is important to organize garden planting to produce a continuous supply of flowers to

keep bees fed throughout spring and summer. Different types of bee prefer feeding on different plants, so you should try to provide a good variety of flowers to appeal to as many types of bee as possible. They tend to prefer wild flowers (richer in nectar than plants that have been intensively bred), although they will be attracted to a wide range of flowers found in many gardens. In winter, British beekeepers feed their honey bee colonies sugar-based solutions or similar honey substitutes.

With bee habitats shrinking at an alarming rate, it's more important than ever that a welcome should be extended to bees in every garden, large or small, town or country, and that every encouragement should be given to persuade them to take up long-term residence.

POPULAR SPRING FLOWERS FOR BEES

- Bluebells
- Daffodils
- Flowering cherry
- Rosemary
- Viburnum

FAVOURITE EARLY SUMMER GARDEN FLOWERS FOR BEES

- Campanula
- Everlasting sweet pea
- Fennel
- Foxglove
- Snapdragon

LATE SUMMER GARDEN FLOWERS FOR BEES

- Aster
- Buddleia
- Dahlia
- Heather
- Lavender

THE PEDIGREE OF HONEY DOES NOT CONCERN THE BEE

EMILY DICKINSON

INSECT ALLIES

Insects such as ladybirds, lacewings, hoverflies and ground beetles can be of great assistance to organic and eco gardeners in controlling pests, especially aphids.

In return for sustenance and shelter in the garden, they will gobble up and destroy huge quantities of plant-damagers; in its brief life a ladybird can account for 5,000 aphids! Not that insect appetites are restricted to small invertebrate pests; the devil's coach horse beetle, for example, is an able predator of slugs and snails.

Gardeners can encourage beneficial insects by stocking their gardens with plants that they find attractive. Many are drawn to common weeds and by striking a workable compromise, maintaining a patch of nettles for example, gardeners can offer plants that insects are attracted to in the wild.

When it comes to choosing suitable flowering plants, try and select ones that will produce flowers for as much of the year as possible.

A wide range will also attract a good cross-section of insects. Among the major aphid eaters, hoverflies are particularly attracted to Limnanthes (poached egg plant), fennel and yarrow – which is also favoured by lacewings and ladybirds. But rather than concentrating on specific plants, eco gardeners are better served by offering a mix of flowering plants to attract insects for as long as possible.

Insects will take up residence in different areas of the garden. Many favour the shelter of long grass, which is a further reason for letting a patch of grass grow wild. Ladybirds will be happy in rough grass underneath a hedge, or in an uncut herbaceous border. Beetles feel at home under rotting logs, a pile of leaves, at the base of a compost heap or in a thick mulch provided it is left undisturbed.

The dense foliage of evergreens and thick hedges makes them attractive to many insects too – as does ivy, which attracts a large number of different species. A lot will also tuck themselves away in well-sheltered habitats when it's time to hibernate.

There are man-made insect homes to supplement or substitute natural accommodation – or why not have a go at making your own? Insects will seek out small, sheltered holes to lay their eggs or hibernate, so you can provide these by drilling lots of small holes in a log and placing it underneath a dense shrub where insects like to feed and shelter. Alternatively cut off the bottom of a plastic drinking bottle, but leave the top, and pack it with drinking straws. Don't remove the cap of the bottle because

having a closed end will stop wind funnelling through the straws as well as keeping out rain. Hang your new insect home in thick foliage.

▲ An 'insect hotel' like the one designed by Sophie Conran for Burgon & Ball can accommodate a wide range of little creatures.

▶ So-called 'wildlife stacks' built into walls or fixed to any garden structure replicate natural features sought by wildlife in your garden – particularly by beetles and other insects.

PRINCIPAL APHID-EATING LARVAE

- Hoverfly
- Lacewing
- Ladybird
- Predatory midges
- Tachinid fly

(Adult ladybirds as well as their larvae eat aphids.)

COMPANION PLANTING

Companion planting is not a new idea: there is evidence that it was practised in ancient times and it is something that should appeal to both the eco and organic gardener.

One underlying principle is that 'companion' plants are deliberately grown alongside those that are prone to attack by insects and other pests, in the hope that the companion plants either repel predators entirely, or prove so attractive to them that they flock to the companion plant and leave the protected plant alone. Companion planting makes no claims to be foolproof, but one thing we can be certain of is that it is chemical-free.

For example, nasturtiums grown beside cabbages are believed to attract caterpillars that would otherwise eat the cabbages. Chervil and coriander are said to deter aphids on lettuce, and dill is similarly said to attract aphid-eating insects. It is thought that onions or chives growing near to carrots mask the smell of the carrots and so deter the dreaded carrot fly. In the same way the powerful scent of French marigolds is credited with deterring a significant number of pests from attacking plants growing alongside them in a greenhouse – plus they also attract hoverflies, which in turn like to eat aphids.

Another equally beneficial side to companion planting draws on the chemical properties of one plant to assist another. Legumes, for example, have long been used to enrich the soil with nitrogen taken from the air, stored in their roots and through them released into the soil. A familiar example of this is the practice adopted by farmers of sowing clover in pastures. Clover fixes nitrogen in the ground to the benefit of grasses that require high levels of this element. On the domestic front, plants belonging to the pea family – lupins, sweet peas and beans – do the same for the benefit of plants growing near them – or for a subsequent crop to enjoy the year after.

▶ Nasturtiums, much beloved by aphids, make excellent companion plants to site alongside other crops that suffer from aphid attack – plus the flowers and seeds are edible and they repeat flower all summer.

Although by no means an exact science, companion planting has the further merit of introducing variety and unexpected combinations of colour, texture and shape to otherwise conventionally planted beds and borders.

COMPANION PLANTING ISN'T FOOLPROOF, BUT IT IS CHEMICAL-FREE

DO-IT-YOURSELF SLUG AND SNAIL CONTROL

Enlisting the help of wildlife to combat garden pests is only one of the measures that the eco gardener can take to protect flowering plants, vegetables and fruit. Slugs and snails can cause serious damage to many plants. Thrushes, hedgehogs, frogs and toads play their part, but by adopting a hands-on policy (literally in a couple of cases) to combat them, or by using home-made traps and barriers, gardeners can take effective measures without the need for pesticides and harmful chemicals.

Slugs look for shelter during the day; many go underground and this is where they are vulnerable to attack by minute worms known as nematodes. These occur naturally in the soil, but parasitic nematodes are specially bred and sold commercially as microscopic slug predators. Mixed with water, the nematodes can be spread over the soil through a watering can, so that they are able to penetrate slugs hiding below the surface and kill them within a few days.

▶ Physical barriers are the most obvious way of deterring slugs and snails. For young plants particularly vulnerable to slug and snail damage, copper collar rings can provide protection.

ON THE SUBJECT OF SNAIL ANNIHILATION VITA SACKVILLE-WEST SAID, 'IT MAY BE UNKIND TO SNAILS, BUT ONE HAS TO MAKE ONE'S CHOICE.'

9 WAYS TO CONTROL SLUGS AND SNAILS

1 Hoe regularly between plants. Eggs of slugs and snails are small and white, usually appearing in clusters. If they are worked up into the sun they will either shrivel up and die, or be eaten by predators.

2 Place grass clippings around susceptible plants. This has the double advantage of acting as a mulch and also providing food for slugs before they reach your plants.

3 Rings of sharp grit laid around plants, either individually, or along both sides (and ends) of the rows, will damage the undersides of slugs and snails and help deter them from venturing further. Alternatively, use broken eggshells, mixed with dry bran, which absorbs the moisture needed by slugs and snails. In fact any rough and sharp material will deter slugs and snails for a while; the important point to remember is that these physical barriers will need to be renewed regularly because they will be dispersed by wind, rain and the movement of other wildlife.

4 Barriers made from prickly plants, like holly or thorn, can also deter slugs and snails. Placed around plants you want to protect, the spiky surface will ward them off. You will need to keep a check on these defences, like the ones above, to make sure they haven't been dislodged.

5 Get chickens!

6 Some gardeners put copper tapes or rings around plants or pots; the copper seems to emit a tiny electrical current that deters molluscs.

7 Another well-tried way of dealing with slugs is to create 'slug pubs': beer traps filled with waste beer. Made from saucers or old lids, beer traps should be sunk into the soil, with the rims protruding just above ground level; slugs will crawl up and over, but beetles will be protected from falling in. Fill with beer and keep them topped up. Slugs love beer, so check all the traps regularly, emptying out slugs that have been lured into them and topping up with beer when the level drops, or after it has rained.

8 Leave pieces of wood, bits of old carpet, or anything else offering shelter, lying about the garden. Slugs and snails will take refuge underneath them and all you have to do is pick up the cover and collect whatever is hiding there.

9 If all else fails … be on the lookout for slugs and snails, especially after a long dry spell. Armed with gloves and torches, you can eradicate visible culprits on night-time garden patrols. Pick up all the slugs and snails you see and either take them well away from your patch, or place them in salt water to kill them and then add them to the compost heap when dead.

▲ Encourage thrushes to your garden by growing berried shrubs. Thrushes are very partial to snails and will smash the snail's shell against an anvil (usually a rock). Blackbirds often steal the snail after the Song Thrush has cracked it open.

MATERIAL MATTERS

Surprising as it may seem, our choice of garden landscaping materials can have an impact on the global environment. That may sound a bit extreme when we're talking about a dozen or so new concrete slabs to make a small patio, but stopping to think through how and where those slabs are made may make us search out more eco-friendly landscaping materials.

Just because we see concrete almost everywhere we look (away from the open countryside), doesn't alter the fact that making concrete uses a great deal of energy, which in turn produces significant quantities of carbon dioxide, thus increasing your carbon footprint. It's fair to say that the concrete manufacturing industry is making efforts to reduce energy consumption and harmful emissions, but when other options are available, new concrete products should still be seen as a last resort.

When it comes to selecting materials for hard landscaping, the answer has to be investigating the impact they have had on the environment during sourcing, manufacture and transportation. If those stack up, then you've done that small bit for the planet.

This kind of thinking isn't restricted to ground-covering materials. A lot of us need fences of one kind or another in, or around, our gardens. But before automatically getting a builder to quote for a new brick or stone wall, or nipping down to a garden centre to load up with panels of larchlap fencing, there are alternatives worth thinking about. A hedge is an obvious choice. Once grown, it provides a screen and it can

THE RAISED BED RETAINERS FEATURED ARE MADE OF RECYCLED MATERIALS AND WERE PART OF THE AWARD-WINNING REAL RUBBISH WILDLIFE GARDEN SPONSORED BY THE RSPB AT CHELSEA IN 2005

also be a wonderful habitat and food source for pest-eating animals, insects and birds. Hedges also form the best kind of windbreaks, because they filter the wind, breaking it up and reducing its force – whereas wind will push up and over a solid wall to form a damaging back swirl on the leeward side.

Hazel hurdles are just as effective as a hedge in filtering strong wind and they have the advantage of coming ready-made. Hazel is also a widely available organic material in this country. Hazel hurdles are easy to install, take up no more space than other panelled fencing, and look at home right away in a garden setting. With practice, you may even be able to make them yourself – and what could be more satisfying than that?

ALTERNATIVE LANDSCAPING MATERIALS

- **Recycled materials** – Second-hand slabs, recycled bricks, cobbles, or stone blocks have a weathered look which would suit any garden.

- **Natural stone** – Locally sourced stone is an ideal construction material. Coming from nearby, transporting it to your garden will keep carbon emissions to a minimum, unlike the high level of carbon released into the atmosphere from transporting stone from more distant sources.

- **Gravel** – Locally sourced gravel is another excellent choice, for the same reason as stone quarried in your area. Some gravel is dredged from the seabed causing severe damage to sensitive marine ecosystems. Distributing seabed gravel to inland customers also increases its carbon footprint as a result of carbon dioxide emissions from its transportation.

- **Wood** – Wood is a fantastic material to use in the garden. It is 100% natural and is a truly sustainable resource. Look out for the FSC logo when purchasing wood. This stands for Forest Stewardship Council and proves that the wood has come from a responsibly managed forest. If possible try to source wood locally; it is far less damaging to the environment than buying wood that has been shipped from the other side of the world. If wood has been treated with preservative to prevent rot, it has also introduced potentially harmful chemicals into the garden – if you can afford a hardwood like oak, which doesn't need preservative, it makes it an even more eco-friendly option.

▼ An eye-catching use of recycled materials is seen in this award-winning garden design where rubber tyres filled with grass have been used to create stepping stones set in a base of crushed bricks.

PEAT

The issue surrounding the horticultural use of peat is extremely contentious and it's one that eco gardeners need to address.

For many years peat has played an important part in the manufacture of commercially produced composts and mulches – establishing itself as a valuable garden material. Peat has a number of things in its favour. To begin with it is wholly organic, derived from a natural source, and when it breaks down it introduces plant nutrients to the soil and supplies food for earthworms. Once wet, peat retains moisture well and releases it slowly, making it an ideal medium for plant roots to grow in. Mixed with soil, peat improves its structure, breaking up densely packed clay soils for example, helping them to drain better, while improving moisture retention in light soils.

Unfortunately its benefits and success have led to a big increase in demand and this has put great pressure on supplies in many countries. Peat is formed from the decomposition of bog plants, principally sphagnum moss, and the

transition from plant to peat can take centuries; much of the peat used today was formed thousands of years ago. Some parts of the world, areas of Canada for example, have very large deposits of peat where developing a sustainable peat mining industry is feasible – although transporting peat to overseas markets adds to greenhouse gas emissions. Smaller peat deposits elsewhere, such as those in the British Isles, do not have the capacity to renew themselves at the rate at which they are currently being used. If peat extraction continues at its present-day level, the existence of peat bogs, their delicate ecosystems and the biodiversity they support are threatened.

Mining peat presents a further environmental problem. Peat bogs contain high levels of CO_2, which is released when peat is extracted and processed for horticultural use – which itself adds to the emission of greenhouse gases.

▶ The success of peat as a gardening material has been its undoing in many parts of the world, where reserves can no longer keep up with demand, leading to the growing use of alternatives from sustainable sources.

It's against this background that efforts are being made to replace peat with alternatives and limit its use to the few tasks where no subsitute has been proven to be as effective. Materials derived from wood – sawdust, wood fibre, composted bark – provide good bulk and excellent drainage properties in alternative 'composts'. Compost from large-scale green waste recycling facilities is a nutrient-rich component in potting composts. Coir, which holds water well, is becoming widely used as a peat substitute. The major snag with coir is that it has to be transported to the UK from tropical countries (principally Sri Lanka) and shipping it causes significant carbon emissions.

The eco gardener can revert to the old-fashioned method of making a well-balanced potting mix for raising plants from equal measures of leaf mould, garden compost and loam. This has the joint benefit of draining well, while also being fertile.

THE RIGHT PLANT IN THE RIGHT PLACE

Every eco gardener will want his or her plants to thrive efficiently without the need for undue attention, repeated watering, or the use of artificial growth stimulants. One way of helping any plant to flourish is to put it in the right place: somewhere that has the right soil conditions and an appropriate balance of sunlight and shade. Given these, a plant will grow healthy and strong, making it more resistant to disease and requiring less input to keep it going.

Although it is possible to grow a plant that needs a lot of water in a dry spot by giving it liberal amounts of water, this wholly contradicts the principle of eco gardening that works to reduce the use of valuable resources like water. The same goes for feeding plants chemicals to sustain them in conditions where they would otherwise perish.

Applying common sense and giving up ideas of trying to achieve something that would never happen naturally will achieve more satisfactory and sustainable results. Plants that could suffer frost damage will need winter shelter and protection. Conducting a simple soil analysis will establish the pH balance in soil, confirming which plants are suited to it and which aren't.

By understanding the needs of our plants and looking after them when they are getting established, they should grow satisfactorily without putting too many demands on us. And if a plant can't survive without constant watering and feeding, we should accept that it's nature's way of telling us that we shouldn't have planted it where it is in the first place.

THIS WONDERFUL EXAMPLE OF DAMP GARDEN PLANTING FEATURES A RANGE OF CAREFULLY CHOSEN PLANTS THAT WILL THRIVE IN THE SHADY DAMPNESS

PONDS

Creating a pond is one of the most valuable contributions an eco gardener can make towards encouraging beneficial wildlife into a garden.

Even a small pond will attract amphibians and insects that need water for part of their lifecycle, as well as providing somewhere for birds to bathe and water for them (and other pest-eating creatures) to drink. With far fewer natural ponds in the UK than there were a century ago, gardeners who put ponds in their gardens are helping to restore very important wildlife habitats.

Constructing a pond is not complicated. It will need a waterproof lining, and if there is a local source of suitable clay, this is the ideal material for a pond in an eco garden as it makes a natural waterproof layer. Spread over the interior of a pond, a 15cm-thick layer of clay will retain water without needing an artificial liner that uses energy (and therefore carbon emissions) in its manufacture. If the pond is done away with at some time in the future, a clay lining will become naturally integrated into the surrounding

soil, whereas an artificial liner will have to be disposed of in the same way as household rubbish. Packing down clay to line a pond does require greater physical effort than dropping in an artificial liner, but the ecological benefits are well worth it.

Ways of saving rainwater are described later, and recycling this to fill and top-up a pond not only benefits plants that colonize it, but it means that tap water won't be needed – which reduces household consumption.

A pond works best if part of it is shaded, to reduce the spread of algae. Creatures need to be able to get to the water easily as well, which is why one edge should have a gentle slope leading from it, ideally fringed with rough grass or plenty of foliage as shelter. If the slope has a firm base made from flat stones, for example, it will provide safe and ready access

▶ A small well-planted pond will give you an added aesthetic dimension to your garden and provide a wonderful habitat for wildlife.

for various kinds of wildlife from hedgehogs to young amphibians. As plants begin to colonize the pond, the number of wildlife residents will increase, attracting predators, which will also begin devouring plant-damaging pests in other parts of the garden.

Weed will need to be removed from time to time, but ponds are best left undisturbed until well into the summer, when taking away dense weed will upset creatures living in it less than it would earlier in the year. If you do scoop invasive plants, leave them beside the pond overnight so that anything gathered up at the same time can slip back into the pond under cover of darkness. Once they're safely back home, you can add the weed to the compost heap.

WATER HARVESTING AND CONSERVATION

Most of us take water for granted. We turn on a tap and we expect clean, drinkable water to flow out – and keep on flowing out. Many gardeners in the developed world only become aware of the amount of water we consume (and waste) when water shortages loom and hosepipe bans are imposed.

Although the volume of water on earth is the same as it has always been, the increasing demand in the developed world is damaging the natural cycle of water distribution. Renewable water resources are becoming over-stretched, leading to supply shortages and the need to extract more water from rivers, which in turn damages their ecosystems. Self-evidently, cutting back on water usage – especially in the garden – is an important step that eco gardeners can take towards preserving and maintaining this vital resource.

Waterwise, 'the leading authority on water efficiency in the UK', (www.waterwise.org.uk),

estimates that half a tonne of water is delivered to every British household every day, and in summer, when additional water is needed, more than half of that extra supply is used outdoors.

Many gardeners use mains water (that's drinking-quality water, remember) to water lawns, flowerbeds, container plants and vegetables, leaving the water companies to collect the rainwater that runs away from our gutters.

This is where the eco gardener enters the picture. By implementing a few straightforward measures, it is possible to cut back significantly on the amount of mains water

▼ Although river water represents only 0.2% of all the fresh water on Earth, it plays a very important role distributing water, organisms and important gases and nutrients. Rivers help drain rainwater and provide habitats for many species of plants and animals.

used in our gardens and replace it with harvested rainwater.

Harvested rainwater is also better for our plants. It does not have the concentration of chemicals (such as chlorine) that are added as part of the treatment process of mains water, which can harm sensitive plants as well as important microbes active in the soil. Rainwater generally has a lower pH than mains water, meaning that it can be used on all kinds of plants. A further advantage of rainwater over mains water is the financial one. Rainwater is free and the less mains water we use, the lower the water bills for people with meters fitted to their supplies.

As the pages that follow explain, we can make further savings in water by selecting plants that are used to living in more arid conditions than many of our familiar garden varieties; this applies especially to the types of grass we grow in our lawns. Allied to this is the efficient use of the water we do give our plants. Are we watering at the most suitable time of the day? Are we giving plants the right amount of water? Are we conserving water in the soil once it has been given to them?

It's only by honestly assessing how we use water in our gardens that we can develop a far more thoughtful, efficient and fundamentally sustainable way of gardening.

▶ Ingenious but practical systems of conveying water around a garden can add interest and tranquillity as well as being a source of water for wildlife unable to access birdbaths.

WATER BUTTS

Any sloping roof – on a garden shed, a greenhouse, or a conservatory, as well as a garage or a house – can be fitted with a gutter and downpipe.

Unfortunately, far too much of the rainwater that flows through our gutters and downpipes runs away into municipal drainage systems. By fitting water butts, though, we can preserve a great deal of this otherwise lost rainwater, which is ideal for watering house plants and topping up garden ponds, as well as providing a vital reservoir during times of water shortage.

The amount that can be saved depends on two factors: the surface area of the roof on which the rain falls and the volume of rain falling. The equation below shows how this can be calculated.

- 1 millimetre of rain to 1 square metre of roof = 1 litre of rainwater

Even on a small scale it can be useful to collect rainwater – and here's why…

- The average annual rainfall in England is 926.9mm

- Take a small garden shed with a roof measuring 1.8m x 1.2m = 2.16sqm
- The amount of water running off that roof every year is 2002 litres
- Every month, on average, that amounts to 166 litres
- And every week the roof of that small shed could produce 38 litres

Now imagine how much water you can collect from the roof of your house! By linking together a series of water butts using diverter pipes it is possible to fill more than one butt from a single downpipe.

With the growing interest in conserving water, some householders are moving beyond traditional water butts and installing rainwater harvesting systems with big underground tanks to capture and retain rainwater on a large scale.

▼ With a one-off investment, capturing rainwater run-off from any sloping roof is the easiest thing anyone can do to ensure a supply of untreated water for the garden.

EFFECTIVE WATERING

Watering plants effectively is another key aspect of eco gardening. By following a few straightforward principles, it's possible to reduce the amount of water needed to keep plants growing healthily while ensuring that water is put to the best possible use.

Suggestions for effective watering include:

- Reduce moisture loss from the soil by preparing it in autumn and winter when rainfall is greatest.

- Help soil retain moisture by digging deep and digging in plenty of organic material.

- Let plants establish good root systems by planting in spring and autumn, before or after periods of dry summer weather.

- Limit the number of hanging baskets – they require a lot of watering.

- Place saucers underneath containers to catch the run-off from watering – this surplus will be drawn back to the container plants' roots when it's needed.

- Remove weeds because they challenge plants for water.

- Check the soil before watering and only water if it feels dry at the depth of the cutting edge of a digging spade head.

- Apply water steadily – through the rose of a watering can for example, as opposed to a gush from a hosepipe – as a steady trickle is less damaging to soil structure.

- Water in the evening or early morning to reduce loss through evaporation.

- Direct water to plant roots by soaking the soil around stems rather than wetting leaves.

- Group together plants that have similar water needs so that they each get the right amount of water.

LOW-WATER PLANTS AND LAWNS

The kind of lateral thinking called for when creating an eco garden should make us consider the kind of plants we grow.

With increasing temperatures and the prospect of longer periods of dry weather, we can save water by choosing plants that can cope with hotter drier conditions than many conventional garden varieties.

Garden centres will be able to give advice on drought-tolerant plants and they will also understand which plants do well in local soil and climate conditions. Plant leaves are good indicators of those that will tolerate periods of heat and drought. These fall into four general categories:

- Leaves with small surface areas (rosemary and lavender for example), which lose less water than larger leaves.
- Those that store moisture or reduce evaporation – waxy leaves, leathery leaves and fleshy leaves such as escallonia and yucca.
- Leaves that reduce the impact of heat – by shading themselves with a hairy surface (like lamb's ears) or by secreting a substance that cools the surfaces of leaves as it evaporates (catmint and sage for instance).
- Silver or grey-green leaves are capable of tolerating hot, dry conditions because the colour reflects the sun's heat. Artemisia and Verbascum are typical examples.

When it comes to planting and maintaining lawns, many grass species are very drought tolerant and most lawns can survive without watering at all in a dry summer. The grass may become parched and yellow, but once the rain returns it will soon become lush and green again. Consider opting for 'mixed' lawns that include clover, which remains greener longer than grass as well as encouraging pollinating insects.

Letting lawn grass grow longer in dry weather and mowing less frequently will keep moisture in the soil. Keeping a lawn well aerated will ensure that when it does rain, water will reach the roots of the grass rather than run off the compacted surface.

IN HER FAMOUS DRY GARDEN IN ESSEX, BETH CHATTO COMBINES PLANTS THAT ARE NATURALLY ADAPTED TO FLOURISH IN DRY CONDITIONS

GREY WATER IN THE GARDEN

Using grey water in the garden is another strategy that eco gardeners can adopt to reduce our overall use of mains water and ease the demand on water resources.

Grey water is the term used to describe water that drains from showers, baths and washing-machines. Used with care, it can supply valuable quantities of water for garden plants.

What determines whether or not grey water is suitable in our gardens is the level of potentially harmful chemicals that come from detergents. By switching to eco-friendly products, the risk to our plants is immediately reduced and if we can get into the habit of using smaller quantities of these products, the risk drops even further. Bath water containing non-eco products can be used occasionally, but regular use in the same area may cause a build-up of chemicals in the soil that could threaten plant health.

TIPS FOR USING GREY WATER

- Recycle bath water. Let it cool and then pump it from the bath straight into the garden using a manual pump and a length of hosepipe.

- Water used for cleaning fruit and vegetables is ideal, but don't use washing-up water.

- Use grey water right away – don't store it.

- Rotate grey water around the garden.

- Don't use grey water on fruit and vegetables that are going to be eaten raw.

- If any plants show signs of stress, make sure that the chemical concentrations in future batches are more dilute.

- Wash your hands after using grey water.

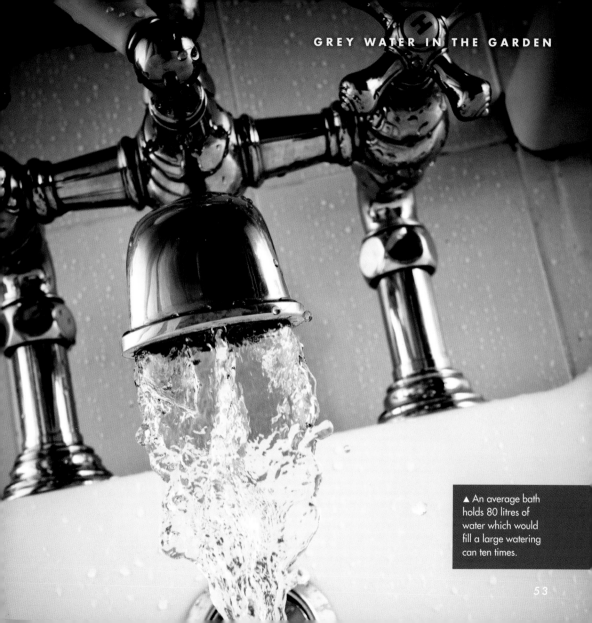

▲ An average bath holds 80 litres of water which would fill a large watering can ten times.

53

MULCHES AND MULCHING

Using mulches is an important part of organic gardening and it's a technique that eco gardeners will want to adopt in the course of developing sustainable, resource-efficient gardening.

Mulches can help gardeners in a number of ways: suppressing weeds, improving the soil and retaining moisture. Some mulches are principally decorative: stone chippings, pebbles and gravel that are often used as mulches around container plants curb the evaporation of moisture from the plant's roots, but they are not placed there to improve the soil or compost in which the plant is growing. By sacrificing visual appeal and choosing organic matter as a mulch, it will act as a soil conditioner, gradually rotting down and introducing nutrients and fibre into the soil while helping to retain water.

Commonly used organic mulches include composted forest bark, compost and home-made leaf mould (both of which are described later). To be effective these need to be spread over the soil in a layer at least five centimetres thick. This will let water percolate through to the soil below and down to the roots of cultivated plants, but it will be thick enough to shield the soil from the drying effects of hot sunshine and wind.

Before applying any of these mulches, however, it is very important to water the soil really well, so that the roots get a good supply of moisture before the mulch is spread. Check the depth of mulches periodically and top them up to maintain the right level of protective cover.

Also don't apply too early in the spring or you will delay the heating up of the soil.

▶ Mulches like bark wood chippings can be usefully deployed in a garden in several ways – as a naturally draining path material that suppresses weed growth or spread over the soil surface around shrubs and trees to maintain moisture and improve soil conditions.

RECYCLING RUBBISH

Most households throw away things that an eco gardener would find very useful and a search through the average dustbin bag is likely to reveal various bits of 'rubbish' that can be recycled and put to good use in the garden.

With a little imagination, ways of giving other bits of 'waste' a second lease of life outdoors may well come to light. The following are just a few of the ingenious ideas that are already in use.

Well-cleaned yoghurt pots and similar containers are ideal for raising seedlings to be given away or swapped. Cardboard centres from rolls of kitchen and lavatory paper can be used in the same way. (See overleaf for details of the brilliantly simple and practical Burgon & Ball Eco Potmaker.)

Use well-rinsed plastic bottles cut in half as mini-cloches to protect individual seedlings,

especially at night (cut holes if necessary, for ventilation).

Old tights or stockings make handy ties for plants and trees.

Used teabags are ideal for putting in the base of flowerpots. They retain moisture, break down quickly and they allow plant roots to develop. When they rot down, they even add a tiny amount of organic matter to the soil.

Mixed in with these there is sure to be a fair amount of uncooked fruit and vegetable waste that could go to the compost heap, as described later.

ECO POTMAKER

This simple kit allows gardeners to make a limitless supply of sturdy but biodegradable pots for seeds, seedlings and young plants. The Eco Potmaker enables you to make pots in three different sizes.

- Decide how big you want your pot to be and cut a strip of paper of the right length and width.
- Roll the strip loosely around the smaller of the two cylinders, leaving paper overhanging to make the bottom of the pot.
- Fold this overhang underneath the cylinder.
- Press together the two halves of the Eco Potmaker.
- Give it a gentle twist.
- Now remove it and your pot is made.
- Fill the pot with compost and seedlings.
- Plant the pot directly into the ground and the paper will break down naturally as it biodegrades.

▲ This very useful paper potmaker kit is produced by Burgon & Ball.

the long-running cartoon. Directo
Phelim McDermott (Shockheaded
European
liquidity
money mar
accounts
Bank said
placed in
an idea.

SEED SAVING AND SWAPPING

Saving and swapping seed combines two fundamental principles of eco gardening: recycling and reducing. Saving seed recycles produce from a previous year's harvest to grow into crops for the next harvest, creating a sustainable circle of regeneration. At the same time it cuts down packaging waste and saves shopping trips to buy packets of seed, which helps conserve energy and reduces carbon emissions. As a further incentive, saving your own seed also saves money; allowing a certain number of plants to flower and set seed will produce a significant number of seeds – more than you are likely to find in a bought packet – and your home-grown seed can be collected for free.

It isn't possible for commercial seed producers to supply seeds of every variety of plant: there are simply too many of them. Inevitably, varieties for which there is less demand cease to be available from large-scale producers and when this happens there is a risk they could disappear. This is where seed banks and swapping seeds between gardeners help preserve plant varieties that are no longer available from commercial sources.

At a national level, Garden Organic (the national charity for organic growing: www.gardenorganic.org.uk) maintains its Heritage Seed Library 'to safeguard rare vegetable varieties, that were once the mainstay of British gardens'. A selection of these seeds are made available each year to members, some of whom have volunteered to grow seed in their capacity as designated Seed Guardians; indeed, almost half the seed made available each year by the Heritage Seed Library is supplied by these volunteers. (A similar seed distribution programme is run by the Royal Horticultural Society for the benefit of its members.)

Initiatives like these play a key part in maintaining biodiversity. For all we know, old varieties may preserve valuable plant genes that could prove to be hugely important in the future, possibly by resisting disease or promoting tolerance to drought – seed swapping has an important place in eco gardening by promoting sustainability. Seed swaps are organized by local gardening groups all over the country and details about many of them can be found on the internet.

In order for seed to be swapped, it must first be stored. This is not complicated, but to do it successfully, it pays to follow certain basic guidelines:

- Seeds need to be stored dry, so collect them in paper bags, not plastic ones, to avoid condensation.
- Choose seed from healthy plants that have good yields.
- Take seed from several plants of the same variety to keep genetic diversity.
- After collection, place seeds somewhere cool and dry for several days, to remove all moisture.
- Reject any small, damaged seeds as well as any showing signs of mildew or disease.
- Make sure seeds are clean and free of all plant debris before being put away in storage.
- Label storage envelopes with the name of the plant the seed was taken from and the date it was stored.
- Keep seeds somewhere cool to optimize germination. Every degree cooler significantly increases the life of stored seed.
- Depending on their variety, seeds can be stored for five years or longer, but check on them from time to time to make sure they are still in good condition.

SEEDS

SEEDS

Burgon

grow your own

SEED STORAGE ENVELOPE
Burgon & Ball

Collected By:

Seed Type:

Date Collected:

Collected From:

Collected By:

▲ Seeds, when interestingly packaged, make great gifts – save and share your favourite varieties of flowers and vegetables with your friends. Enhance the seed packet with your own photos.

63

COMPOSTING

If any single gardening activity embraces all the principles of eco gardening, it has to be composting. By giving nature a helping hand, nature repays the compliment by recycling unwanted vegetation, kitchen waste and grass cuttings, to produce rich brown, sweet-smelling, crumbly compost that is a boon for the soil and plants in any garden.

By following a simple process you can reduce the costly disposal of household and garden waste, retain and recycle valuable nutrients, and return them to your garden to the benefit of everything growing there. Composting at home not only saves money that would otherwise be spent on soil 'improvers', bought composts, fertilizers, mulches and chemicals designed to enhance the health of plants – not to mention the fuel used to go and buy them and carry them home – but it also helps reduce the amount of household waste that has to be transported to municipal refuse centres or, worse still, sent to landfill sites. Instead of burying organic waste in land that could be put to more productive use and where it produces harmful greenhouses gases, composting is the perfect way to cut waste and benefit in the process.

Home-made garden compost is the ideal natural soil conditioner, fertilizing the soil, improving its structure and also serving as a valuable mulch – suppressing weeds and retaining moisture. Rich in plant nutrients and mineral trace elements, it's an excellent plant food, that can be dug into the soil to give new plants a healthy start, or spread on the soil as a top-dressing where it will slowly release nutrition to established plants.

GARDENING IS ABOUT GIVING AND TAKING – WELL-ROTTED GARDEN COMPOST IS ONE OF THE THINGS YOU CAN GIVE BACK

Making compost requires very little equipment and as much work as a gardener wants to put into it; most of the recycling process is undertaken by worms and micro-organisms living in the garden. The 'turn-around' time from raw waste to crumbly compost depends on how much waste material you have, how you compost it and how much time you choose to spend on the process. Whether it takes a few months or a year, though, the results are always hugely satisfying.

▶ Composting is not necessarily a pretty business but anyone who is even half a gardener will forfeit space, appearance and effort for the booty!

BALANCE AND MIX IN COMPOST

Compost is made in a heap. Heaps may come in different shapes and sizes, but fundamentally a successful compost heap creates an environment in which worms and microscopic organisms can get to work and thrive. To do this they need three essential elements: air, water and food. If they have these, they will keep eating organic waste thereby converting it into compost.

Composting materials can be divided into two groups, often referred to as 'greens' and 'browns'. To produce compost, 'greens' (soft, wet materials) need to be mixed with drier, tougher materials – the 'browns' – which rot down more slowly. 'Browns' also provide fibre in compost, which gives it a good structure.

It's worth knowing that these 'greens' and 'browns' also represent two important chemicals that are crucial to the composting process. 'Greens' are rich in nitrogen, 'browns' are rich in carbon – and getting a good balance of these lies at the heart of making compost successfully.

The Centre for Alternative Technology has devised a very effective analogy for a good compost mix: the cheese sandwich. The two slices of bread in the sandwich represent the 'browns' – the much thinner slice of cheese equates to the 'greens'.

Although there may be a chemical formula for the ideal compost mix, you can get the

▶ Commercial accelerators can be added to your compost to aid the speed at which decomposition occurs, but a cheaper and equally effective way is to ensure that the material put on your heap is well shredded, which enables the worms to penetrate the mass of material more easily.

SLOW-ROTTING 'BROWNS' INCLUDE:

- Dried leaves
- Hay
- Natural fabrics
- Sawdust
- Torn-up cardboard such as toilet roll centres, egg boxes, cereal cartons
- Small woody prunings, such as hedge trimmings
- Straw
- Wood ash

QUICK-ROTTING 'GREENS' INCLUDE:

- Kitchen vegetable waste
- Grass mowings
- Soft green prunings
- Comfrey leaves
- Nettles
- Green leaves
- Old bedding plants
- Seaweed
- Wool

correct balance of 'greens' and 'browns' by watching what happens to your compost as it rots down.

- If the compost starts to go wet and sloppy, add more 'browns'.
- If it looks dry, add more 'greens' *and* don't forget to water the heap.

It's best to avoid putting perennial weeds such as bindweed, docks and ground elder on your heap. It only needs a little piece to survive the composting process and it will start to grow again. The best way of dealing with perennial weeds is to send them to a council recycling centre where composting methods will be hot enough to kill them.

Tough, woody plant stems can be added to a compost heap, but they should be chopped into small pieces first to help them break down quicker. For the eco gardener, the ideal tool for doing this is a sharp spade, which avoids the need to use electricity, petrol or diesel to drive a powered shredder.

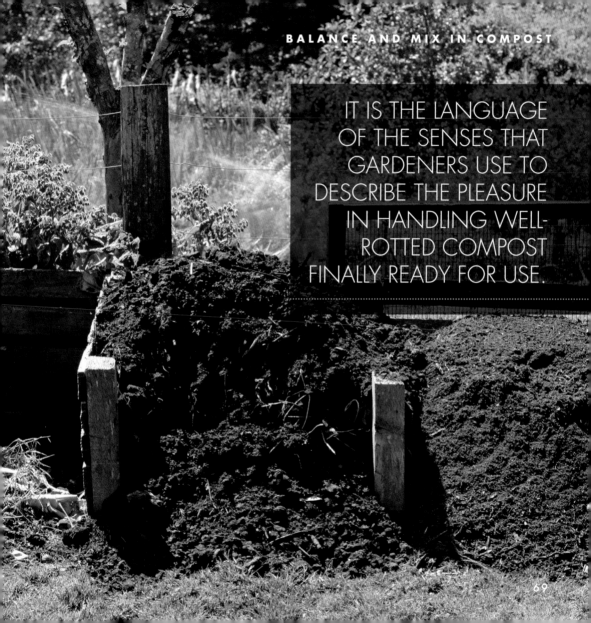

IT IS THE LANGUAGE OF THE SENSES THAT GARDENERS USE TO DESCRIBE THE PLEASURE IN HANDLING WELL-ROTTED COMPOST FINALLY READY FOR USE.

MAKING COMPOST

Whether you choose to build a free-standing compost heap or opt for a bin or box (described later), your heap will need to sit directly on the ground to allow worms and other compost-making creatures in the soil to gain access to it. To that end, your first task should be to fork over the ground to make it easier for them to move into the heap – doing this will improve drainage as well.

Heat generated by aerobic microbes breaking down organic material is the key to making compost and the more heat that can be generated, the faster compost will be made. Successful heaps are built with a flat top, or sides, over which sacking or old carpet can be laid as insulation.

You should aim to construct it in layers, so that you get a good mix of materials all through the heap, helping air and moisture circulate inside it. The bottom layer should be soft twiggy material, about 20cm deep. On top of that should be five centimetres or so of unrotted material from the top or sides of an earlier compost heap; if you don't have that to hand a layer of soil will do just as well. On top of this will go alternate layers of 'greens' and 'browns' 20 to 30cm deep, until the heap is a little over one metre high.

Gardeners with a lot of suitable waste – and the right balance of 'greens' and 'browns' – can build a compost heap in one session. This is the fastest way of making compost (because the heap will generate an impressive amount of heat in just a few days), but it only suits people who are able to amass the right balance of material. Most gardeners create compost heaps gradually, adding organic material as it comes to hand.

▶ Worms play a key part in breaking down organic material in a conventional compost heap.

If the weather is dry, material at the sides and edges of a compost heap will soon dry out, and so will benefit from being watered to keep it moist. After a few days, a heap that is working well will sink and when this happens more material can be added in layers as before.

You can check on how your compost is progressing by digging into your heap a couple of times a year. The lower part should comprise rich, friable compost. On top of this will be layers in various stages of decay, while the topmost layers will be made up of the most recently added organic material, which will only just have started to rot down. To extract the compost that has already formed, fork out the upper layers, dig out the compost, then mix up and pile back all the unrotted material, leaving it to be converted into compost as additional layered organic material is added. That's really all there is to it.

Well … almost all. If you have the energy and inclination to turn the contents of a heap two or three times, it will noticeably speed the composting process. Keep an eye on it, watching as the heat generated inside by the activity of aerobic microbes causes the material to compress and sink. (You can use a specially designed compost thermometer to get an accurate reading.) As the heap sinks, oxygen flowing through it will reduce, as will the level of microbe activity, causing the heap to cool. By turning the contents you increase oxygen flow, boost the microbes into action again and raise the heat level to speed the breaking down of organic material that produces compost.

Turning involves forking out all the material, mixing it up and piling it back into a heap, making sure that what was on the outside is placed in the middle, closest to the centre of heat. In addition to improving oxygen levels, turning compost blends material and gives the gardener a chance to look inside a heap and check on its condition.

There is no denying that turning compost requires considerable effort. Fortunately compost aerators have been developed to mix up compost in a similar, but less tiring, way by stirring up the contents of the heap, creating gaps through which air can pass carrying oxygen right through it.

However, turning and aerating is by no means essential and if you don't mind waiting for compost to form, simply adding organic material to a heap without touching it further is a perfectly acceptable and efficient method. It's entirely up to you – either way, making compost at home is a richly rewarding experience.

There is one additional step that can be taken to speed the process, whether or not you turn your compost: adding an accelerator. This is packed with active bacteria, which give a kick-start to your composting by helping organic material decompose quicker than it would in normal composting conditions. The best accelerators are 100% organic and produce compost richer in nutrients and of far higher quality than conventional methods.

THE FRUITS OF YOUR
LABOUR – FROM
GARDEN AND
KITCHEN WASTE TO
RICH, FRIABLE, SWEET-
SMELLING COMPOST
READY FOR USE TO
ENRICH THE SOIL

COMPOST CONTAINERS

There is nothing wrong with making compost in a free-standing, flat-topped, heap; though making compost in a bin or box has the advantage of keeping the heap (and your garden) looking tidy.

Some gardeners build compost containers using wood, wire netting, concrete blocks or bricks. Others opt for commercially made pre-fabricated bins or boxes.

Easy access to the compost is important and a commonly used design comprises three fixed sides of a bin with a fourth side made from horizontal boards fitted into vertical slots either side of the opening. This arrangement allows the boards to be lifted in and out individually to remove compost, add organic material, or turn the heap (if that is what you decide to do).

An alternative is provided by constructing a container from 'layers' placed on top of each other as a heap grows, or removed as it shrinks and the compost is ready to be used. This kind of compost bin is often made from wooden boards and resembles a square beehive when the layers are stacked together. An even simpler method

makes use of old car tyres to create a series of circular layers piled on top of each other.

For those with enough space in their garden and enough organic material to make use of more than one container, a popular design is the New Zealand box. This often comprises three wooden boxes, each with a removable front, and together they enable a gardener to keep up a constant momentum of recycling. One box is dedicated to new organic material, which is added until the box is full. The second box contains a full heap that is in the process of being composted. And the third box has a heap of compost ready for use in the garden.

Then there are a variety of plastic bins and containers, many of which are made available by local authorities at very attractive prices to encourage home composting. These are ideal for recycling smaller quantities of organic

▼ Neat, tidy and functional – three-box compost systems suit gardens with plentiful supplies of organic material, providing a constant cycle of compost through the systematic and simultaneous use of all three boxes.

waste. Most have some form of lid, for filling the container, and some are fitted with a door at the bottom for extracting compost. All except compost tumblers (below) sit directly on top of the soil and once in place using them is simply a matter of dropping in the right balance of material and leaving the rest to nature.

As their name suggests, compost tumblers work on the principle that the container is regularly turned on its pivoted frame. Garden and kitchen waste is placed inside the tumbler, to which are added a few trowels of finished compost or garden soil to get the process started. Some gardeners prefer to add a compost accelerator packed with useful bacteria to kick-start the process, because unlike methods where the compost is in contact with the ground, enabling worms to work into the organic material, the breakdown of waste in a tumbler relies on the microbe activity from the added compost, soil or accelerator. Turning the tumbler several times a week ensures that the organic material inside remains well aerated and well mixed.

▶ Whichever container you use to make compost, the raw materials remain the same: a good mixture of quick-rotting 'greens' and slower-rotting 'browns'.

LEAF MOULD

There was a time, not so long ago in some cases, when fallen leaves were regarded as a nuisance that had to be raked into piles before being consigned to a bonfire. Fortunately attitudes have changed and the full benefit of recycling them is widely appreciated among organic and eco gardeners.

Left to nature, fallen leaves will gradually decompose to produce a rich, dark material that has a variety of uses. Nature will do the same to leaves gathered together by a gardener. It may a take a year or two for this to happen, but once leaves have been collected and put somewhere to rot down, the gardener can forget about them until the resulting material is ready for use.

The principal purpose of leaf mould containers is to keep leaves together in a tidy heap month in, month out, as they gradually rot down. Provided a container does that, it can be made from comparatively lightweight materials and many gardeners use a structure of wire netting and wooden stakes.

Simpler still are leaf composting sacks. Once these are filled with leaves, they just need to be tied at the top and stacked at the bottom of the garden for a year, until the leaves have formed a useful mulch, or for a couple of years, by which time the leaf mould should have turned into a valuable soil conditioner. Mixed with loam and sand, it is also an excellent top-dressing for lawns.

Leaves from most deciduous trees can be used to make leaf mould, particularly ones with a high tannin content, such as oak and beech leaves. The only ones that are best avoided are those from evergreen trees like conifers, holly and laurel, which take longer to rot down.

IT HAS OFTEN BEEN POINTED OUT THAT THE GARDENER BURNS HIS INHERITANCE ON THE GARDEN BONFIRE

CHRISTOPHER LLOYD

WORM CASTS AND ORGANIC FERTILIZERS

The natural fertilizer produced by the action of worms in a wormery has a two-fold benefit for the eco gardener. It reduces the use of chemical fertilizer while also recycling kitchen waste and household scraps.

The worms at work in this process are brandling, or tiger, worms, which are found in piles of decaying leaves, manure and compost heaps. They produce two forms of fertilizer in a wormery: a solid (their rich dark casts) and a liquid.

You can buy custom-made wormeries that come supplied with worms to get you started. The essential feature of all wormeries is that the surplus liquid produced as the worms break down organic material drains down to a reservoir in the base.

Worms need a few days to settle in to a damp bedding layer of compost, torn-up newspaper, or rotted sawdust before small amounts of kitchen and vegetable waste are introduced and they get to work.

Organic material is added, small amounts at a time, and it can take twelve months for a wormery to get up to full production.

The rich, dark worm cast 'fertilizer' starts to appear after a few months. In order to extract it, the top layer of partially decomposed waste, which contains the worms, will need to be scooped out and put carefully to one side.

▶ There are many wormery designs but a basic principle applies to them all. Worms are the essential and most efficient tool in rotting down organic matter, turning household and garden waste into a valuable garden fertilizer.

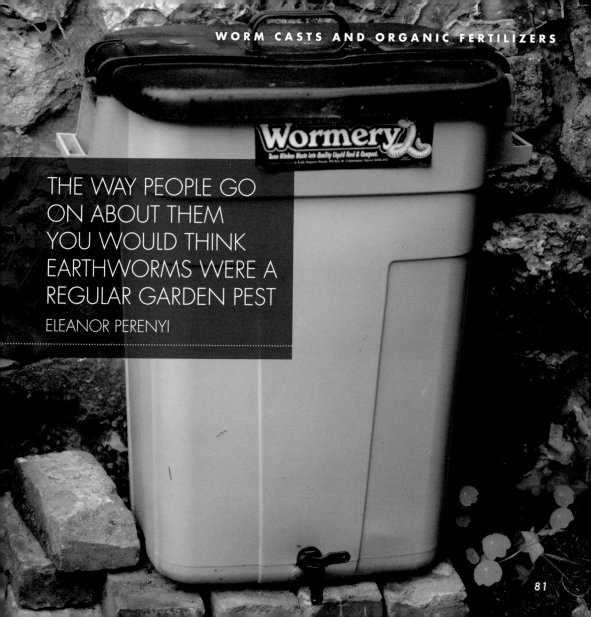

THE WAY PEOPLE GO
ON ABOUT THEM
YOU WOULD THINK
EARTHWORMS WERE A
REGULAR GARDEN PEST

ELEANOR PERENYI

With the worms safely out of the way, the worm casts can be scooped out as well. After that, the layer of waste containing the worms can be returned to the wormery, where they can carry on their work with fresh supplies of organic waste.

Since worm casts are rich in nutrients, only small quantities need to be used to nourish plants. They make a very good top-dressing for container plants and a useful fertilizer in a potting mix.

The liquid that collects at the base of a wormery needs to be drained off from time to time. Diluted with water (10 parts water to one part wormery liquid), it is a good plant food. Alternatively it can be poured over a compost heap to provide moisture and nourishment to the creatures at work there.

Wormery liquid is just one of the organic fertilizers that gardeners can make at home. Nettles and comfrey can both be used to make excellent natural plant feeds – they do have a strong smell, however.

The most nutrient-rich nettles for making a general liquid plant feed are young ones cut in spring. Freshly cut nettles should be steeped in water for two weeks, using a ratio of a bucketful of nettles to 10 litres of water. When the liquid is ready, it needs to be diluted in the same proportions: one part liquid nettle feed to 10 parts water.

Comfrey produces a liquid feed that is particularly good for use on fruiting plants such as tomatoes, aubergines and cucumbers. The feed is made by filling a bucket half full of comfrey leaves, adding water until the leaves are covered then placing a lid on top. Leave for 3–5 weeks. When ready the comfrey liquid can be used undiluted (but be warned – the mixture will become a bit whiffy!).

Comfrey leaves can also produce a concentrated feed. Leaves are stuffed into a container that has a lid and a hole in the base, through which a dark liquid will begin to seep after 15–20 days. This should be diluted with water in a ratio of 1:15.

► Organic fertilizers are available to buy if you don't have time to make your own.

grow your own

100%
ORGANIC
POTATO
FERTILIZER

1.5KG
(enough to fertilize approx. 30 potato plants!)

Burgon & Ball
SHEFFIELD ENGLAND

GROW YOUR OWN

Growing your own food in a way that is efficient and sustainable is one of the great rewards of eco gardening. Home-grown fruit and vegetables can go straight from plot to plate – with no storage time and no loss of vitamins and taste. They can be brought to the table without clocking up food miles, with no need for packaging and quite probably without chemical input. Raised from seed stored and recycled from a previous year's crop, grown with the aid of home-made compost, and watered with captured rainwater, eco garden produce embodies the values of low-impact, sustainable food production.

Successfully growing garden produce has never been easier; in fact you don't even need a garden. Anyone with a small area of outdoor space – a patio, a terrace, a window sill, even just a wall on which to hang a vertical planter – can grow herbs, salad crops, tomatoes and vegetables – even potatoes in containers.

Since eco gardening looks for ways of avoiding waste of any sort, sharing your home-grown produce with friends and family ensures that lots of people have the chance to enjoy vitamin-packed fruit and vegetables fresh from the garden.

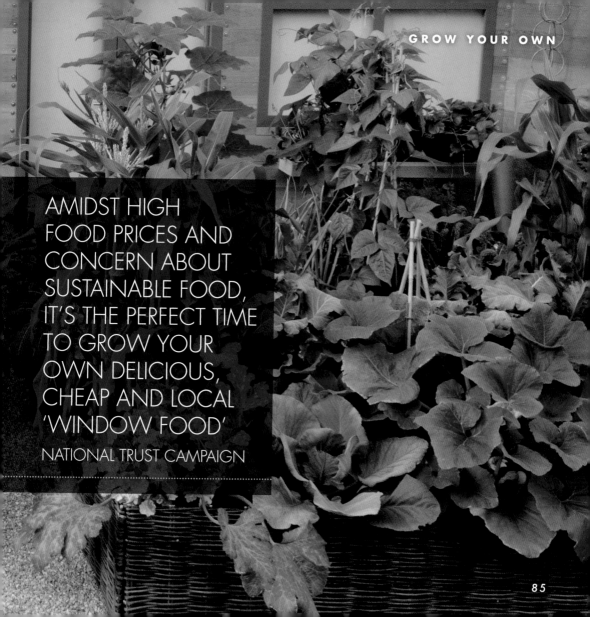

AMIDST HIGH
FOOD PRICES AND
CONCERN ABOUT
SUSTAINABLE FOOD,
IT'S THE PERFECT TIME
TO GROW YOUR
OWN DELICIOUS,
CHEAP AND LOCAL
'WINDOW FOOD'

NATIONAL TRUST CAMPAIGN

HOME HARVEST

After growing garden produce, the eco gardener can relish the satisfying process of preserving and storing away supplies of fruit, vegetables and herbs for the lean months before the garden begins to yield food once again. This cuts down on groceries that have to be bought, so reducing packaging brought into the house and the fuel needed to go and buy them – all of which help minimize the eco gardener's carbon footprint.

These days freezing is the most widely used method of preserving home-grown produce, because it retains the flavour and colour of freshly-picked food. Most vegetables freeze well, the exceptions being salad crops and tomatoes, which will break down if frozen whole. However, tomatoes can be frozen successfully if they are first reduced to a purée.

Most vegetables require blanching before they are frozen. This process destroys enzymes in the vegetables, which would cause them to deteriorate in the time they take to freeze and then thaw before being used. Blanching takes place once vegetables are cleaned and prepared for freezing. They need to be lowered into boiling water – which needs to be brought back to the boil as quickly as possible – left in it a for set period of time depending on what is being blanched (information available at websites such as www.allotment.org.uk), then immediately plunged into iced water to stop them cooking further. When the food has cooled it should be drained and then mopped dry with absorbent kitchen paper before being bagged and labelled for freezing.

Most UK-grown fruits will freeze well. With care, the following can be frozen and then unfrozen with their skin structure more or less undamaged: gooseberries, bilberries, blueberries and currants (black, red and white). Apples, though, do require blanching. However, it is more efficient (saving time and using less freezer space) to freeze fruit in the form of purées, sorbets or ice cream.

Pickling is suitable for red cabbage, cauliflower, mushrooms, onions, green tomatoes, nasturtium seeds, beetroot, gherkins, courgettes and marrows. Many of these vegetables can also be made into tasty chutneys.

Making jams and jellies remains one of the most popular ways of preserving fruit. It is relatively simple to do and the results will last throughout the year. Home-made preserves in decorative jars also make welcome gifts for friends and family.

Legumes (peas and beans) that have grown too large to be eaten fresh can be slow dried. In late autumn when cold, dank weather comes, and rot starts to develop, the whole plant can be uprooted and hung upside down in a dry, airy place. The more mature, well-developed pods will dry out to allow their contents to be stored in dry containers. This works well with runner and French beans, as well as peas.

Pick herbs – early in the morning to preserve the oils in them – and dry for use in the winter. Why not dry camomile flowers and mint leaves to make your own herbal teas?

RASPBERRY JAM

You'll need equal weights of raspberries and sugar. Heat slowly in a preserving pan, stirring until all the sugar is dissolved. Boil hard for 3 or 4 minutes, then transfer into prepared, sterilized jars and seal when cool.

For an interesting variation, try using 75% red currants and 25% raspberries in this recipe; the red currants will take slightly longer to cook, so begin by softening the fruit in a little water over a low heat before you add the sugar.

IN *THE HOUSEWIFE'S WHAT'S WHAT* PUBLISHED IN 1904 IT WAS CLAIMED THAT 'HOME-MADE JAMS ARE FAST GOING OUT OF FASHION.' 100 YEARS ON THEY ARE ALL THE RAGE AGAIN!

TOOLS TO LAST

In a throwaway society the eco gardener comes up against the widespread tendency to buy cheap garden tools and equipment in the mistaken belief that this is the way to work a garden economically.

However, it only takes a few frustrating afternoons struggling with badly designed and poorly made tools to realize they are a false economy. The eco gardener, with an eye on avoiding waste and making the best use of materials, should quickly appreciate that buying tools made with real quality not only saves money in the long run, but the investment is repaid with years of comfortable, pleasurable use – with a well-made tool serving a lifetime of gardening, instead of a succession of low-cost, disappointing and poorly performing throwaways.

A digging spade with a hardened and tempered steel head, substantial strapped socket, ash shaft and ergonomically designed handle, for example, will be more expensive than a cheap substitute – but which will be in use for years to come? For the eco gardener there is no contest. Where other spades will clog in the soil, quickly tire the digger and possibly snap under a winter's toil, a well-designed and expertly made spade like the one described above will move easily through the heaviest ground, bringing speed and satisfaction to any garden job.

Choosing garden tools and other equipment is a matter of personal preference and well-made tools merit careful consideration before one is selected and paid for. Tools need to be handled by the user to make sure they feel comfortable and will continue to feel comfortable year in, year out. Using good tools is something every gardener should look

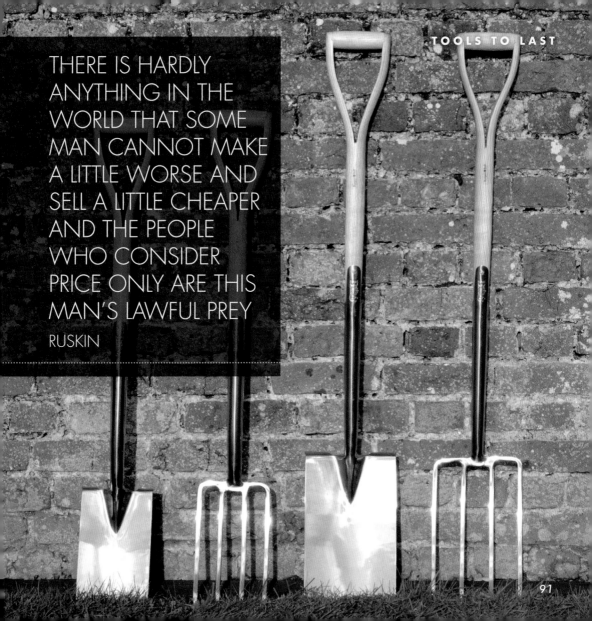

THERE IS HARDLY
ANYTHING IN THE
WORLD THAT SOME
MAN CANNOT MAKE
A LITTLE WORSE AND
SELL A LITTLE CHEAPER
AND THE PEOPLE
WHO CONSIDER
PRICE ONLY ARE THIS
MAN'S LAWFUL PREY

RUSKIN

forward to. If they feel right and function well, gardeners will also be encouraged to look after them and keep them in tip-top condition.

Some of the qualities built into the best-made tools are:

- Handles and shafts made from (sustainable sources of) hardwood. Ash, for instance, is strong and has excellent shock-absorption properties.

- Handles that feel good in the hand. There are three types of handle for tools such as forks and spades, shaped like the letters D, Y and T. These refer to the way the handle is connected to the shaft of the tool. Many gardeners find T-shaped tools tiring after a while, whereas Y- and D-shaped handles tend to be more comfortable to grip and work with.

- Small details can reflect build-quality. Using the example of a digging spade again, it's instructive to look at how the top of the head is designed. If there are treads along the upper edge, they will make pushing down on the spade with the sole of one's feet significantly more comfortable than it would be if the head was left as just a narrow strip of steel.

- Sharp cutting edges: when it comes to cutting tools, they need to be razor sharp to cut cleanly and reduce the risk of disease entering plants; those with top-quality heat-treated, high-carbon steel blades will keep their edge longest. Secateurs and garden knives must be the right size to feel comfortable in use, with the best secateurs having cushioned handles.

Good tools will remain good tools providing they are cared for – cleaned of earth and plant debris, oiled and hung up in the dry after use. Those that need to be sharp should be kept sharp to maintain clean cutting edges and avoid putting undue strain on their moving parts. Looked after properly, the best quality tools will return years of satisfying, problem-free gardening.

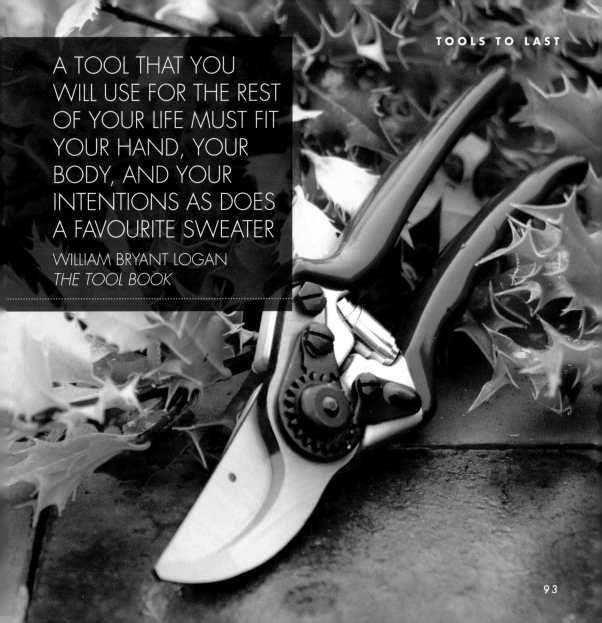

A TOOL THAT YOU WILL USE FOR THE REST OF YOUR LIFE MUST FIT YOUR HAND, YOUR BODY, AND YOUR INTENTIONS AS DOES A FAVOURITE SWEATER

WILLIAM BRYANT LOGAN
THE TOOL BOOK

COMPOSTABLE

PEELINGS TEA BAGS EGG
SHELLS

Burgon & Ball manufacture a wide range of products to help you to garden in a more environmentally friendly way.

For more information visit www.burgonandball.com

USEFUL LINKS AND RESOURCES

The following websites contain further information on the subjects covered in this book:

The Big Wildlife Garden
www.bigwildlifegarden.org.uk

The British Beekeepers Association (BBKA)
www.bbka.org.uk

The British Hedgehog Preservation Society
(BHPS)
www.britishhedgehogs.org.uk

Buglife – The Invertebrate Conservation Trust
www.buglife.org.uk

Centre for Alternative Technology (CAT)
www.cat.org.uk.

Garden Organic
www.gardenorganic.org.uk

Hedgehog Bottom Rescue
www.hedgehog-rescue.org.uk

The National Biodiversity Network (NBN)
www.nbn.org.uk

recycle-more
www.recycle-more.co.uk

The Royal Horticultural Society (RHS)
www.rhs.org.uk

The Royal Society for the Protection of Birds
(RSPB)
www.rspb.org.uk

The Royal Society of Wildlife Trusts (RSWT)
www.wildlifetrusts.org

The Soil Association
www.soilassociation.org

Waterwise
www.waterwise.org.uk

First published in the United Kingdom in 2012 by Burgon & Ball
Packaged by Susanna Geoghegan

© Copyright 2012 Brandreth Partnership

The pulp in the paper used in this book comes from known and
responsible sources.

Printed in China.

ISBN: 978-0-9558456-1-1

Design by Milestone Design

The photographs in this book have been reproduced courtesy of:

Burgon & Ball, pages 1, 24, 49, 58, 59, 63, 79, 83, 85, 87,
89, 91, 93 and 94

Harpur Garden Images, pages 3, 7, 19, 25, 27, 29, 33, 35, 39,
41, 45, 47, 51, 55, 57 and 75

Ardea, pages 15, 17 and 31

Centre of Alternative Technology, pages 9, 21 and 73

Hedgehog Bottom Rescue, page 11

FLPA, page 81